The Adventures of
Ahmi Tsunami

ABC's Matter!

Alex J. Appel

ISBN: 1729698921
ISBN-13: 978-1729698921

DEDICATION

To Ahmi.

ABC's Matter!

Learning Your ABC's

ABC's this way!

The letter A is for:

Ahmi

Aa

And Air Plane!

The letter B is for:

Bulldozer

4

The letter C is for:

Cactus

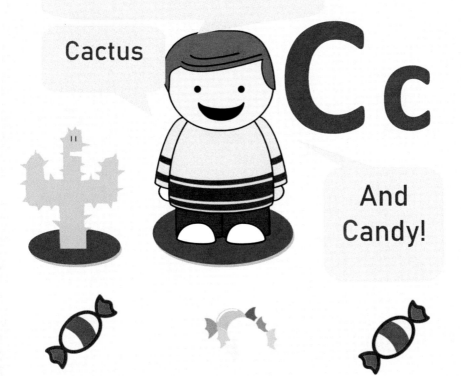

Cc

And
Candy!

The letter D is for:

Dinosaur

Dd

The letter E is for:

Elephant

The letter F is for:

Funnel Cake

Yummy!

The letter G is for:

Girl

Gg

The letter H is for:

Hh

Honey

HONEY

I i

The letter **I** is for:

Ice cube

The letter **J** is for:

Jungle

J j

The letter K is for:

K k

Kindergarten

The letter L is for:

L l

Learning!

The letter M is for:

Money

Mm

The letter N is for:

Numbers

Nn

Oo

The letter O is for:

Octopus

The letter P is for:

Penguin

Pp

The letter Q is for:

Queen

Qq

The letter R is for:

Rainbow

Rr

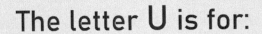

The letter U is for:

Unicycle

U u

The letter V is for

Volcano

V v

The letter W is for:

Whistle

W w

The letter X is for:

X-ray

X x

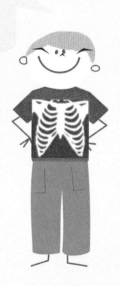

The letter Y is for:

Yodel

The letter Z is for:

Zebra

Thank you for learning with me.

I am excited to learn my Number's with you next time!

Practice ABCs Here:

Practice ABCs Here:

This page is intentionally left blank.

69147492R00015